Ethan Allen

Revolutionary Hero

Colonial Leaders

Lord Baltimore
English Politician and Colonist

Benjamin Banneker
American Mathematician and Astronomer

Sir William Berkeley
Governor of Virginia

William Bradford
Governor of Plymouth Colony

Jonathan Edwards
Colonial Religious Leader

Benjamin Franklin
American Statesman, Scientist, and Writer

Anne Hutchinson
Religious Leader

Cotton Mather
Author, Clergyman, and Scholar

Increase Mather
Clergyman and Scholar

James Oglethorpe
Humanitarian and Soldier

William Penn
Founder of Democracy

Sir Walter Raleigh
English Explorer and Author

Caesar Rodney
American Patriot

John Smith
English Explorer and Colonist

Miles Standish
Plymouth Colony Leader

Peter Stuyvesant
Dutch Military Leader

George Whitefield
Clergyman and Scholar

Roger Williams
Founder of Rhode Island

John Winthrop
Politician and Statesman

John Peter Zenger
Free Press Advocate

Revolutionary War Leaders

John Adams
Second U.S. President

Ethan Allen
Revolutionary Hero

Benedict Arnold
Traitor to the Cause

King George III
English Monarch

Nathanael Greene
Military Leader

Nathan Hale
Revolutionary Hero

Alexander Hamilton
First U.S. Secretary of the Treasury

John Hancock
President of the Continental Congress

Patrick Henry
American Statesman and Speaker

John Jay
First Chief Justice of the Supreme Court

Thomas Jefferson
Author of the Declaration of Independence

John Paul Jones
Father of the U.S. Navy

Lafayette
French Freedom Fighter

James Madison
Father of the Constitution

Francis Marion
The Swamp Fox

James Monroe
American Statesman

Thomas Paine
Political Writer

Paul Revere
American Patriot

Betsy Ross
American Patriot

George Washington
First U.S. President

Famous Figures of the Civil War Era

Jefferson Davis
Confederate President

Frederick Douglass
Abolitionist and Author

Ulysses S. Grant
Military Leader and President

Stonewall Jackson
Confederate General

Robert E. Lee
Confederate General

Abraham Lincoln
Civil War President

William Sherman
Union General

Harriet Beecher Stowe
Author of Uncle Tom's Cabin

Sojourner Truth
Abolitionist, Suffragist, and Preacher

Harriet Tubman
Leader of the Underground Railroad

Ethan Allen

Revolutionary Hero

Virginia Aronson

Arthur M. Schlesinger, jr.
Senior Consulting Editor

Chelsea House Publishers

Philadelphia

Produced by 21st Century Publishing and Communications, Inc.
New York, NY. http://www.21cpc.com

CHELSEA HOUSE PUBLISHERS
Production Manager Pamela Loos
Art Director Sara Davis
Director of Photography Judy L. Hasday
Managing Editor James D. Gallagher
Senior Production Editor J. Christopher Higgins

Staff for *ETHAN ALLEN*
Project Editor/Publishing Coordinator Jim McAvoy
Project Editor Anne Hill
Associate Art Director Takeshi Takahashi
Series Design Keith Trego

The Chelsea House World Wide Web address is
http://www.chelseahouse.com

First Printing
1 3 5 7 9 8 6 4 2

Library of Congress Cataloging-in-Publication Data

Aronson, Virginia.
    Ethan Allen / Virginia Aronson.
        p.   cm. — (Revolutionary War leaders)
    Includes bibliographical references and index.
    ISBN 0-7910-5974-X (hc) — 0-7910-6132-9 (pbk.)
        1. Allen, Ethan, 1738-1789—Juvenile literature. 2. Soldiers—
    United States—Biography—Juvenile literature. 3. Vermont—Militia
    —Biography—Juvenile literature. 4. Vermont—History—Revolution,
    1775-1783—Campaigns—Juvenile literature. 5. United States—
    History—Revolution, 1775-1783—Campaigns—Juvenile literature. [1.
    Allen, Ethan, 1738-1789. 2. Soldiers. 3. Vermont—History—To 1791.
    4. United States—History—Revolution, 1775-1783.] I. Title. II. Series.

    E207.A4 A76   2000
    973.3'092—dc21
    [B]   00-038381
                                                         CIP

Publisher's Note: In Colonial and Revolutionary War America, there were no standard rules for spelling, punctuation, capitalization, or grammar. Some of the quotations that appear in the Colonial Leaders and Revolutionary War Leaders series come from original documents and letters written during this time in history. Original quotations reflect writing inconsistencies of the period.

Contents

Ethan Allen was born on a Connecticut farm on a winter day in 1738. He loved the woods and country-side and as a boy had many adventures there.

Frontier Boy

According to the legend still told about the birth of the Revolutionary War leader and Vermont hero Ethan Allen, a bitter wind whistled through the thick trees in Litchfield, Connecticut, on the night of January 21, 1738. While snow blew into drifts as tall as the roofs in that backwoods village, and wolves howled from the deep forest surrounding the isolated hamlet, Mary Baker Allen gave birth to her first child. The infant's father, Joseph Allen, chose a name from the family Bible for his newborn son: Ethan.

Although the story may be exaggerated, Ethan's

birth in the cold winter of colonial Connecticut can be seen as symbolic of the life he was to lead. Ethan was a backwoodsman who loved, claimed, and tamed the frozen **frontier** forest lands of early America. From the start, he thrived on nature, danger, and using his wits to survive—and win.

Before Ethan turned two, the Allens moved to Cornwall, Connecticut, a brand-new **township**, or crude frontier community, where Joseph had purchased some farmland. The Bible was pulled from the mantel over the fireplace six more times as Ethan's new brothers and sisters were born: Lydia, Heman, Heber, Levi, Zimri, and Ira. Only Lucy Allen seems to have received a non-biblical name.

Although the growing family regularly attended the Episcopal church in Cornwall, Joe Allen was known as a heretic—a person who publicly disagrees with officially established religious beliefs. Joe was outspoken in his disapproval of the strict rules and restrictive ideas of **Calvinism**, a **Puritan** doctrine that had great influence over much of the population of the American colonies in the mid-1700s. Little Ethan was deeply influenced by his freethinking father's ability to question authority and speak out for what he believed while keeping the respect of his peers.

In the early American colonies, children worked alongside adults, accomplishing the many chores required for survival. Backwoods boys had to work very hard, fishing and hunting, trapping wild animals for food and furs, cutting down trees for firewood, and walking everywhere—sometimes on cleared trails, more often through the thick, dark woods.

Unlike most other frontier boys, young Ethan liked reading as well as being a brave woodsman. He read the Bible over and over until his neighbors began lending him their books. Supposedly, young Ethan borrowed—and read—every book in Cornwall. Before long, Ethan's father sent him to the neighboring town of Salisbury to be formally schooled by the learned Reverend Jonathan Lee.

The Allens planned to one day send Ethan to Yale College. That plan ended when Joe died unexpectedly in 1755. Ethan returned home to help bury his father and take over as head of the Allen family. His education and his boyhood were over.

Taking charge of the farm, young Ethan kept the family finances in order and provided for his mother and siblings. Although there are no records or portraits of Ethan, legend has it he was the tallest man in town, towering a head above six feet. He was powerfully built, muscular, energetic, and smart. The strong young man plowed and planted, trading produce for provisions his family desired, such as salt, pepper, and tea.

When he was 19, Ethan turned the farm over to his brothers. Excited by the prospect of travel and adventure, he joined a **militia** regiment of British and American men and became Private Ethan Allen. Britain and France were at war, fighting over American land that both countries

**A battle scene from the French and Indian War.
Ethan had hoped to fight in the war but instead
came home without seeing any action.**

claimed belonged to them. Ethan's troop was
sent to defend a New York fort against an attack
by French soldiers.

The militia marched north to Lake George but
arrived too late to save the fort. The regiment

marched back to Connecticut. Before long, young Ethan's brief enlistment and unremarkable involvement in the French and Indian War ended. Ethan was very impressed by, and always remembered, the stark beauty of the northland, the wilderness that lay beyond the Connecticut borders.

In 1761, Ethan started a business. He built a blast furnace to begin **smelting** iron ore into pure iron. His was the first full-fledged ironworks industry in Connecticut. Ethan's venture rapidly became a very successful business. Iron was in wide demand at that time for use in making kettles. In later years, the blast furnace would also make the iron for equipment required by American soldiers, and Ethan would be helping the **Yankee** cause in even more remarkable ways.

By the spring of 1762, Ethan was a well-regarded businessman with a number of employees, as well as a landowner with a steady income. One day in June, he rode his horse into

Ethan worked hard and built a successful iron works business, which later produced equipment for the American soldiers to use to fight the British.

the nearby town of Roxbury and got married. His new wife, Mary Brownson, was one of 11 children, the daughter of a miller. She was deeply religious and completely humorless, in sharp contrast to her new husband. Ethan was a merry, hard-drinking heretic, who was known to swear so loudly and joke so crudely that other men would fall silent. If Mary disapproved, she probably did not see her unorthodox husband often enough to influence him. Ethan spent most of his time during their 20 years of marriage away from home.

In 1763 Ethan and his wife moved to a small farm he had purchased in Salisbury, which was near his iron operation. Twelve years into their marriage, a daughter was born to the couple. They named her Loraine.

By 1764, Ethan's booming business had grown to more than 50 employees—but he was beginning to grow bored. A backwoodsman at heart, Ethan's enthusiasm for purchasing mines and selling iron was gone.

During this time, Ethan kept his philosophical and imaginative mind stimulated through his friendship with a local physician, Dr. Thomas Young. Like Ethan, Dr. Young was an avid reader, a heretic, and an original thinker. He also had the best personal library in the area, and the two spent a great deal of time together at the Salisbury tavern, drinking "flip," an alcoholic punch, while discussing theology, philosophy, and politics. The two barroom philosophers began to collaborate on a book, a manuscript that would not be published for over 20 years.

Dr. Young showed Ethan how he wrote, printed, and circulated his ideas. Dr. Young published pamphlets in which he attacked the stodgy theories of the masses, who still believed in devils and witchcraft and readily gave up their personal power to the church. He also shared with Ethan his pamphlet on the New Hampshire Grants. This was a controversial area of land located between New Hampshire and New York. Young's impassioned essay included the phrase "Liberty and Property, the household gods of Englishmen." (In the 1760s, American men still considered themselves Englishmen, as the colonies were ruled by Britain at the time.)

In 1749, the governor of the British-owned province of New Hampshire began selling large parcels of unsettled land located west of the Connecticut River. By "granting" such "townships"—at modest fees—he created what would one day be the state of Vermont.

The western boundary of the Grants had not been well established, so New York's governor also claimed the same land and sold it for large sums. The king of Britain backed the New York governor, who demanded additional fees from the Grant settlers—most of whom were backwoodsmen or old soldiers. As a result, a bitter and bloody real estate war was started.

Ethan heartily agreed with Dr. Young.

The heresies of Ethan and Dr. Young did not go unnoticed. In colonial times, one could be arrested, fined, or even imprisoned for publicly expressing different ideas. So Ethan found himself in trouble with the law on a number of occasions. In July 1767, for example, he was physically thrown out of the religious town of Northampton, Massachusetts. He had been inspecting a lead mine there and visited a local tavern, where he loudly poked fun at the ideas of the area churchmen.

It is no wonder that Ethan began to consider making a move northward, to the unsettled land where no laws governed free thinking. He had marched through part of the Grants during his stint with the militia. He also had begun to hear stories from his Connecticut friends about the clear rivers full of fish and the quiet woods rich with game. They were buying up acres and acres of the wild land. In fact, so many men from Connecticut eventually moved to the Grants that, in the mid-1770s, the new state of Vermont was almost named "New Connecticut."

In the winter of 1767, Ethan set out in snowshoes for the steep hills of the distant northern country. Leaving his wife, daughter, and baby son, Joseph, behind on the farm he had purchased in Sheffield, Massachusetts, Ethan hiked into the Green Mountains. It was a trip that would change his life—and the course of American history.

Love of the wilderness spurred many early Americans to continually move onto unsettled land. Ethan took his family to the rugged Grants area when his hometown in Connecticut became too crowded for him.

Green Mountain Boy

Ethan's brother Ira recorded a few stories that became popular legends about Ethan as the ultimate woodsman. According to Ira, his super-strong brother would catch deer by chasing them until they collapsed in exhaustion. Another of the legends tells of one winter day when Ethan got caught in a cold rain as he hiked through the woods. With nightfall came a blizzard, and Ethan's wet clothes froze to his body. The experienced woodsman knew that he could not go to sleep because he would surely freeze to death if he stopped moving. So Ethan marked out a circle in the snow, which he trudged around and around, all through the dark hours. Ethan staggered and fell more than once. Each time, he forced himself to continue marching, which saved his life. He later referred to this dreary night as "among the greatest hazards" of his adventurous life.

On his first solo trip to the Grants, Ethan traveled through deep forests, trapping wild game and listening to the howl of the wolves. Like many other frontiersmen, Ethan fell in love with the great untouched wilderness. Compared to the Grants, Connecticut–with more than 150,000 residents–was too crowded.

Soon after his return to Cornwall, Ethan learned of the first official real estate battle on the Grants. A headstrong resident named James Breakenridge refused to pay fees to New York for the farmland he had already purchased from New Hampshire. New York officials sent out surveyors to claim the land. An angry mob armed with long rifles greeted the men from New York, also known as **Yorkers**, as they arrived. When one of the Yorkers, a justice of the peace, called upon the armed men to disperse, Breakenridge responded, "I hope you will not try to take any advantage of us for our people do not understand law." And they stood their ground.

The Yorkers retreated.

Upon hearing of the Breakenridge confrontation, Ethan rode his horse to the Grants, where he purchased about a thousand acres of land in the area under dispute. He bought up lots in the townships of Poultney and Castleton. Then he rode on to Albany, New York, to attend court hearings on the Breakenridge land and eight other Grants cases. The Yorkers planned to kick out all of the residents who refused to pay their fees. Because the presiding judge, the lieutenant governor of New York, the attorney general, and many other high officials had purchased disputed Grants land themselves, they did not act in a fair and impartial manner.

At a tavern near the courthouse, John Tabor Kempe, the attorney general of New York,

Ethan and his Green Mountain Boys fought to protect their land from New Yorkers before they fought the British.

offered Ethan a generous plot of New Hampshire Grants land if he would convince the others that New York was in the right.

"Sir," responded Ethan, "the gods of the hills are not the gods of the valleys."

His poetic response became famous, and Ethan surely repeated it many times himself at the new tavern in Bennington. Built near the top of a hill, the two-and-one-half-story barroom served as the unofficial town meeting hall for Bennington— and much of the rest of the Grants. To vividly illustrate the political views of most of his bar patrons, landlord Stephen Fay erected a 20-foot pine pole in the dooryard and mounted the tavern's symbol: a stuffed **catamount**. The huge wildcat's ferocious fangs were bared in a fierce snarl, and the savage mountain lion was positioned facing the New York border a few miles to the west. It served as a symbol of the defiant stance shared by most of the people living on the Grants.

In the dimly lit taproom, backwoodsmen drank a lot of **"grog"** and "stonewalls" (strong alcoholic drinks made with rum and hard cider). Joined by the newest Grants landowners who had yet to move in from Connecticut, the regulars at the Catamount were often fired up, fueled with a deadly mixture of alcohol and anger. A group soon formed who agreed that, if need be, they would use force to defend the land against the hated Yorkers. Ethan was elected the colonel commandant, leader of the rugged, ragtag, **minuteman**-style military association. If it had not been for these backwoods volunteers, some 100 militiamen—including Ira and several other Allen brothers—it is likely that Vermont would now be a part of New York.

When the acting governor of New York, Cadwallader Colden, was informed about the "mob" of unruly men in Bennington, he threatened to drive the lot of them into the Green Mountains, or the hills of Vermont. Ethan's militia responded with cool creativity by scoffing loudly before naming themselves "the Green Mountain Boys."

In July 1771, more than 100 armed Yorkers marched toward the Breakenridge farm with the intent of evicting the stubborn farmer and his family. A call went out from the Catamount, and the Green Mountain Boys were rounded up by messengers who rode from farm to farm shouting, "a wolf hunt, a wolf hunt."

When the Yorkers arrived at the Breakenridge place, they faced some 40 armed men backed by what looked like hundreds more peering down at them from a nearby ridge. Most of the frightened Yorkers began to slink away. But their leader, Sheriff Ten Eyck, and a small group of followers approached the farmer's log house. After Ten Eyck read aloud the eviction notice from New York, the 40 Green Mountain Boys raised their rifles and took aim at the small posse.

Once again, the New Yorkers retreated.

By late 1771, Ethan had been declared an outlaw by New York officials, who placed a reward on his head. They were outraged because Ethan and his group had continually harassed the land surveyors from New York, capturing and threatening them before letting them loose to retreat and complain. Most surveyors refused to work in the Grants anymore, and those law officers who attempted to protect their fellow Yorkers were beaten and battered by Ethan and the Green Mountain Boys. To illustrate his fearless defiance, Ethan posted a copy of the reward poster for himself inside the Catamount taproom, alongside another poster he drew that offered payment for the capture of the New York attorney general.

Ethan spent a considerable amount of time at the Catamount, plotting strategy and writing essays and editorials for the *Connecticut Courant*, a Hartford newspaper that supported the people of the Grants in their fight against the Yorkers. He wrote of the "Women sobbing and lamenting, Children crying and Men pierced to the heart with sorrow and indignation at the approaching tyranny of New York"; and of the "hard labouring peasants . . . cultivating a howling wilderness." Meanwhile, Mary Allen waited patiently back in Sheffield for her outlaw husband to plow up some Grant land and move his own family into the beautiful wilderness.

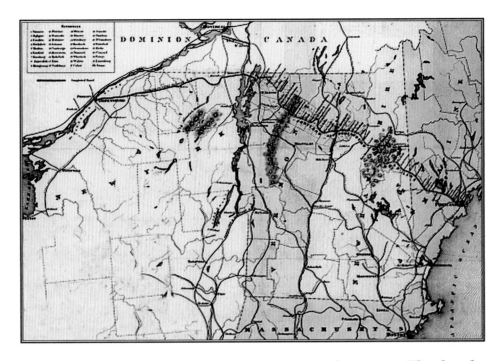

An early map of the New England region. The land that became Vermont was coveted by New York, New Hampshire, Massachusetts, and Canada.

Eventually, Mrs. Allen and the children, including two more daughters, Lucy and Mary Ann, were settled in a small house in Sunderland. If home life in Connecticut and Massachusetts had been difficult, a family's survival in the "howling wilderness" of the Grants was a day-to-day struggle against the odds. Frontierswomen were said to resemble dark-skinned Native

American women, as their pale skin typically turned black from the smoke and soot of constant fires in the hearths of log cabins. Cold and hungry, the women and children were forced to fend for themselves whenever their men left for long stretches of time to hunt, trap, or fight.

By 1773, Ira, the Allen brother with a head for business and a nose for valuable real estate, had organized a family corporation with his brothers Ethan, Heman, and Zimri, as well as their cousin Remember Baker. Within two years, their enterprise, "Allen and Baker," also commonly referred to as the

As the Green Mountain Boys fought to keep their land in what would one day be Vermont, the other colonists had begun to revolt against the British. Willing to use violence, American men banded together to form militias.

On the New Hampshire Grants, a king's court was held in Westminster to collect fees from the settlers. About 100 people protested at the courthouse on the night before one such meeting. A British sheriff and his men, after getting drunk at a nearby tavern, attacked the courthouse protesters and killed one of them. Many Vermonters believe that the incident on this day, March 13, 1775, marks the first bloodshed of the American Revolution.

Onion River Company, had bought up more than 60,000 acres of Grants land. Much of their new land was along the Onion (now Winooski) River where it flowed into Lake Champlain. Soon this area would have a busy harbor. The company advertised plots of prime land for sale in the *Connecticut Courant,* attracting many new settlers to the northland. And the brothers bullied and intimidated any Yorkers who made the mistake of attempting to settle on their land. "My authority is this gun," Ethan loudly proclaimed, scaring off all the New York **squatters**, "and we are a lawless mob."

American colonists fight a skirmish with the British, April 19, 1775. On that day, the Battles of Lexington and Concord in Massachusetts marked the start of the Revolutionary War. When Ethan and the Green Mountain Boys heard the news, they marched south "on a big wolf hunt."

The Big
Wolf Hunt

Early in 1775, the *Connecticut Courant* published a 200-page political pamphlet. Written during weeks of isolation at the Catamount, Ethan's famous treatise had a title that ran almost a full page: *A Brief Narrative of the Proceedings of the Government of New York Relative to Their Obtaining the Jurisdiction of that Large District of Land to the Westward of the Connecticut River* . . . and so on. Ira declared the essay "invaluable in educating the people of other colonies and uniting our people at home." The New York officials had published a number of tracts to present their side of the debate, so Ethan responded in kind.

On March 13, 1775, the Yankees' rebellious stance toward British authority drew blood during the massacre at Westminster. Only a few weeks after that, the American Revolutionary War began in earnest: in Massachusetts, more lives were lost in bloody battles at Lexington and Concord. Untrained Yankee farmers, who called themselves minutemen, faced scarlet-uniformed British soldiers, whom the Yankees called "redcoats." The minutemen were vastly outnumbered and in need of ammunition if they were to maintain the colonies' sudden, violent uprising against Britain.

In early May 1775, the Green Mountain Boys met at the Catamount to discuss what they might do to assist in the revolt. Although the Grants were not regarded as one of the 13 American colonies, the Boys sided with the minutemen—fellow farmers wishing only to live with their families on the land they had paid for, without having to pay additional large sums to an already-wealthy royalty.

Legend has it that, following a long night of drinking and loud declaration, Ethan stood up and announced to the rowdy group, "By God, by God, I'd like to take that fort."

The fort he was referring to was Fort Ticonderoga, on the western shore of Lake Champlain. The British-held fortress housed guns, cannons, and military supplies that could help the Americans win their fight in Boston. No one was really sure how many British soldiers were at "Fort Ti." But the Green Mountain Boys were not afraid. A siege sounded just perfect to them.

The Green Mountain Boys received an official approval from the newly self-appointed colonial authorities, who had formed a congressional war committee in Hartford, Connecticut. Ethan and the Green Mountain Boys shouted, "We're going on a big wolf hunt," as they rode northward through the wilderness, rapidly amassing an army of backwoodsmen and farmers.

In Castleton, which was on the Grants and 20 miles away from Fort Ti, more than 60 soldiers from Connecticut and Massachusetts joined upwards of 150 Green Mountain Boys at a formal meeting. The troops elected Ethan to lead the upcoming siege, and strategy was discussed. Boats would be required to transport the men to the western shore of the huge lake, so volunteers were sent to several nearby British posts to steal the boats.

Ethan and his soldiers were armed with only **muskets** (an early type of shoulder gun) and hunting knives. While they waited for the boats, a surprise visitor rode up: Benedict Arnold, the leader of a Yankee militia. He had been sent by the Massachusetts leaders to capture Fort Ti. Handsome in his gold-buttoned uniform and accompanied by his own valet (personal assistant), Arnold must surely have been an unusual sight in the wilderness outpost.

Even though the Massachusetts committee had made Arnold a colonel and presented him with an official commission to seize the British fortress, the Green Mountain Boys flatly refused

Colonel Benedict Arnold, who was sent to capture Fort Ticonderoga but had to watch as Ethan led the attack.

to participate unless Ethan led the attack. Outraged but helpless to change the troop's decision, Arnold was forced to accept Ethan's offer to join his defiant band of men. Thus, in the early morning hours of May 10, 1775, it was Ethan who led the attack on Fort Ticonderoga.

A few years after the attack, Ethan wrote of the thoughts and emotions that inspired him to lead the first offensive action in the American Revolution: "Ever since I arrived at the state of manhood and acquainted myself with the general history of mankind, I have felt a sincere passion for liberty."

Originally called Fort **Carillon**, the 75-year-old massive stone and wood structure had been designed by French engineers to protect thousands of soldiers. When the British captured the French **garrison** in 1763, they renamed the fort

Like Ethan, Benedict Arnold was from Connecticut. But unlike Ethan, Arnold was a rich merchant who preferred a lavish lifestyle. In 1775, Arnold led a small militia of "gentlemen of influence" from New Haven to fight against the British. He quickly rose through the ranks to become a general in the American army.

Despite his victories during the war, Congress investigated Arnold's actions. Insulted by accusations of dishonesty, General Arnold became a spy for the British. His name continues to be synonymous with treason.

"Ticonderoga," an Indian word meaning "the place between two waters."

At the time of the Green Mountain Boys' attack, only 50 British soldiers guarded the old fort. This was fortunate because Ethan's men found only two boats, so just 83 of the 200 men were able to get to Fort Ti for the attack. As Ethan later remembered, during the final moments before the assault he provided a rousing pep talk:

Friends and fellow soldiers, You have, for a number of years past, been a scourge and terror to arbitrary power. Your valor has been famed abroad. . . . I now propose to advance before you, and, in person, conduct you through the **wicket-gate**; for we must this morning either quit our pretensions to valor, or possess ourselves of this fortress.

Historians doubt that the leader of the Green Mountain Boys actually gave the brilliant last-minute speech he claims to have made. But in the very earliest days of the fight for an independent America, Ethan and his brave Yankee troops successfully captured an important British fort.

Entering through an outer wall that had been ruptured and never repaired, Ethan led his men straight inside to the wicket-gate guarded by a solitary soldier. The surprised sentry fired his gun point-blank at Ethan, but the piece failed to discharge. A second British sentry suddenly appeared, lunging with a bayonet. Ethan cracked the soldier on the head with the flat of his sword, knocking the stunned fellow to the ground. Grateful that his life had been spared, the dazed sentry led Ethan, with Arnold beside him, to the quarters of the fortress commandant.

Captain William Delaplace, who had been paying more attention to his vegetable garden than to the security of the fort in his command, was not immediately available to greet the visitors. His second in command, Lieutenant Jocelyn Feltham, stepped out of the barracks clad in his undergarments. The embarrassed

At Fort Ticonderoga, Ethan surprised the British lieutenant commander, Jocelyn Feltham, who was roused from bed and didn't have time to get dressed.

lieutenant demanded to know by what authority property belonging to King George III was being assaulted.

With the line that would be memorized by countless Vermont schoolchildren in the years to come, Ethan replied, "In the name of the Great

Jehovah and the Continental Congress."

Captain Delaplace then came out of his quarters, presumably after having taken the time he needed to put on his full uniform, but not in time to save the fort under his command. Ethan's small troop had already rounded up and disarmed all of the other British soldiers. Because the surprise had been so complete, not a single shot had been fired. In fact, except for the sentry with a headache from Ethan's sword slap, no one had even been hurt. So, without further delay, the British captain presented Ethan–completely ignoring Benedict Arnold–with his sword in a gesture of surrender.

"The sun seemed to rise that morning with a superior lustre," Ethan wrote of the daybreak that followed his groundbreaking victory. A storied moment in American history had just occurred as, in a matter of 10 minutes, the first British position in the American Revolution was captured. To celebrate the occasion, the Boys invited themselves down into the private cellar of Captain Delaplace, where 90 gallons of excellent-quality rum was attacked with the same enthusiastic spirit as Fort Ti had been.

While the remainder of the Yankee troops landed by the boatload on the shores of the fort throughout the morning, countryfolk from the farms nearby joined the merry soldiers in their rum-fueled victory party. A cannon was fired off in a blast so loud that, legend has it, five unconscious Yankees were immediately revived from a drunken stupor to finish out the party on their feet.

On the day after the seizure of Fort Ti, Ethan's cousin, Remember Baker, and a band of men rowed up to Crown Point, a small British garrison a few miles to the north. Neglected, but brimming with ammunition, Crown Point was easily captured from the nine unsuspecting British soldiers who were stationed there. Again, no shots were fired and no one was hurt. In time, the 200 cannons and other artillery confiscated from Fort Ti and Crown Point would prove instrumental in enabling General George Washington to drive

Colonial troops hauling big guns that had been captured at Fort Ticonderoga. The cannons later helped George Washington drive the British out of Boston.

the redcoats out of the city of Boston.

On May 12, Captain Delaplace, Lieutenant Feltham, and the other captured soldiers were sent under guard to Hartford as prisoners of war. That same day, a formal letter was forwarded from Fort Ti to the Committee of War at Hartford, acknowledging the use of 90 gallons of rum "for the Refreshment of the Fatigued Soldiary," and requesting that the British captain be reimbursed. On June 23, Delaplace signed a receipt for the "Eighteen Pounds Eleven Shillings & Nine Pence Lawful money" due him—as requested by his courteous captor, Ethan Allen, whom some had begun to regard as a sort of Yankee version of Robin Hood.

A panoramic view of Montreal, Canada. Ethan and his men had hoped to capture the city with a bold attack. Instead, they were taken prisoner.

4

Lone Wolf

The fall of the two British forts was a thrill to the colonists and helped build up their sagging spirits. Perhaps, the American **patriots** reasoned, their very own farmers, hunters, backwoodsmen, and merchants would indeed prove to be a match for the fierce British forces. But Ethan's reign as a famed military strategist turned out to be short-lived.

Word soon reached Massachusetts and Connecticut of several unfortunate events in the northland. After soldiers led by Colonel Benedict Arnold overran a small British military operation at St. John's, a base in the lower-lake region, Ethan's troops volunteered to occupy the captured post. Against Arnold's advice, Ethan led about 100 of the Green Mountain Boys over rough waters to the riverbank across from St. John's. Once there, the exhausted men fell asleep without posting sentries. At daybreak the Green Mountain Boys were shocked awake when a massive regiment of British soldiers opened fire on them from the opposite shore.

No one was seriously wounded, but most everyone felt that Ethan had made a terrible military blunder—the first of two foolish mistakes. This one would lose him the chance to become an American Revolutionary War officer, while the second would cost him his freedom.

By early June, Ethan's heart was set on leading a military invasion of Canada. As a result of the reports he had been receiving from his spies and messengers, Ethan had become convinced that the British-ruled city of Montreal had been left practically defenseless. The French Canadians and many of the Indians living in the area were against British rule. Ethan thought these people would surely come to the aid of the Green Mountain Boys if they attacked the British in Montreal. "A vast continent must now sink to slavery and poverty, bondage and horror," Ethan wrote of British-held Canada, "or rise to inconquerable freedom, immense wealth, inexpressible **felicity**, and immortal fame."

Enthused by his own writings and the easy victory at Fort Ti, Ethan was anxious to invade Montreal. But he had not yet been given the necessary military authority by the Continental Congress. Ethan's brother Heman had been appointed a captain, and Ira was a first lieutenant. But, when the Yankee campaign to attack Montreal was officially launched in late summer, Ethan was forced to settle for the role of **civilian** scout, recruiting Canadians along the way to fight against the British rulers.

American troops march in the snow. Due to bad weather, extra soldiers could not arrive at Montreal in time to help Ethan.

Unable to restrict himself to a non-leadership position, Ethan convinced his inexperienced recruits to join him in an unauthorized, surprise attack on Montreal. With a population of nearly 9,000, the Canadian city was one of the largest on the continent. Confident anyway, with his 110 ill-equipped farmers marching along behind him, Ethan advanced quietly toward the sleeping city on the night of September 24, 1775.

While waiting just outside the city for his backup troops—a contingent that, for unknown reasons, never arrived—Ethan began to realize that he had made another big blunder. Over 300 British, Canadian, and Native American soldiers poured out of Montreal, ready to do battle with the American invaders. Many of Ethan's recruits ran off. Only 38 brave men stood beside Ethan when he faced down the enemy soldiers who so outnumbered his own. During the two-hour battle that followed, just two British soldiers were killed, and little more than a dozen men were wounded. "I never saw so much shooting result in so little damage," Ethan remarked later.

Historians have come to the conclusion that, if the backup troops had appeared as planned,

Montreal would probably have fallen. As Ethan's spies had informed him, the city was not heavily armed and, at the time, Canadian officials were intimidated by the success of the American military movement just across the border. But fate was not kind. Ethan lost out on his last chance to become an official military leader. "I thought to have enrolled my name in the list of illustrious American heroes, but was nipped in the bud," he wrote afterward.

Ethan and his sad little band were taken prisoner and herded through the streets of Montreal, marched before a huge crowd of curious Canadians, French, and Indians. In the records of the Canadian Military Command, one impressed official said of the unusual sight: "that uncouth illiterate backwoodsman . . . presented a strange appearance wearing as he did a deerskin fur cap adorned with an eagle's feather, coarse homespun clothing and heavy cowhide hobnailed boots of the rudest make."

This lively commentary was wrong in one

sense: Ethan was not illiterate. In fact, he would one day write quite beautifully about his three years spent under military arrest. *A Narrative of Col. Ethan Allen's Captivity, Containing His Voyages and Travels,* the book based on his experiences as a prisoner, would become a best-seller. It was a masterpiece of adventurous storytelling laced with morale-boosting lines. It charmed the American patriots from its publication in 1779 through many subsequent editions.

But, as Ethan would later describe in gory detail, his years as a prisoner were extremely difficult. His reputation had preceded him, and he was treated with either extra hostility or special care, depending on whether the British officer in charge resented or respected Ethan's brief but widely known military career.

Ethan spent his first five weeks of prison life on board the *Gaspée,* a schooner-of-war. There, he was locked into 30 pounds of iron shackles and forced to use a crude wooden chest for a chair and a bed. Shipped downriver, he was next transferred to the England-bound *Adamant*. On this boat he was housed in a small, bedless pen crammed with 33 of the men who had been captured with him at Montreal. Informed that they were to be hanged upon their arrival in England, the prisoners underwent much physical and emotional abuse on the 40-day trip.

The filthy, depressed prisoners were then marched through the streets of Falmouth, England, which were lined by jeering crowds. They were housed at Pendennis Castle for several weeks before being transferred onto yet another British ship. The group barely escaped the gallows because of the last-minute intervention of King George III. The king decided that the men should be sent home instead. Aboard the frigate *Solebay*, Ethan and the others were further cheered to note that their treatment had noticeably improved. The weary men had been officially proclaimed prisoners of war and were no longer to be abused like common criminals.

After a month at sea, the *Solebay* stopped off

Ethan and his fellow prisoners spent many dreary and miserable months being held captive on one British ship after another.

at Cork, Ireland, where Ethan discovered, to his delight, that he was regarded as a hero. The town took up a collection, donating clothes, suitcoats, tea, and sugar to each of the grateful prisoners. Ethan, as the much-admired conqueror of Ticonderoga, also received some cash, plus, according to his own record: "eight fine Holland shirts and socks ready made, with a number of silk and worsted hose, two pairs of shoes, and two beaver hats, one of which was sent me richly laced with gold . . . wines of the best sort, spirits, gin, loaf and brown sugar, tea and chocolate, with a large round of pickled beef, and a number of fat turkeys."

Unfortunately, the ship's captain decided that, except for the new clothes, the ship's crew should be the ones to enjoy the Irish bounty. Ethan was able to conceal a few gallons of the liquor he had been given, and his spirits were significantly lifted as well by the kindness and hero worship displayed by the people of Cork.

After landing off Cape Fear, North Carolina, the prisoners were moved aboard the *Mercury*, where their poor diet led to an outbreak of **scurvy**. By the time the men were transferred to a city jail in Halifax, Nova Scotia, only 14 of the original group were left. Ethan, like the rest of the exhausted men, had grown very

A draft of a declaration sent by Congress to the British general William Howe, objecting to the harsh treatment of Ethan Allen.

weak. His previously excellent health was failing. Even when he was once again a free man, he would never fully recover his former strength and vitality.

The last of the king's prison ships the men would have to endure was the *Lark*, where Ethan was fairly well treated, provided with a comfortable berth, and invited to join the captain in his cabin at mealtime. "This was so unexpected and sudden a transition," Ethan later wrote, "that it drew tears from my eyes, which all the ill usage I had before met with, was not able to produce."

By the end of 1776, Ethan was placed on parole in the British-held New York Harbor area. Confined to lower Manhattan and later to Long Island, he was allowed to find his own lodgings and roam about within a restricted area. He spent much of his time in the local taverns, amusing the other men with tales of war and captivity.

Not surprisingly, Ethan quickly grew bored and wildly frustrated that he was still unable to participate in the ongoing war. After receiving word that his 11-year-old son Joseph had died of smallpox, Ethan's deep grief added to his great frustration. He began to break parole, repeatedly and openly traveling about in off-limits areas of New York City.

Captured and thrown into the Provost Jail in lower Manhattan, Ethan spent eight months behind bars. On May 6, 1778, in exchange for an American-held British officer, Ethan was officially released after 32 months of imprisonment. "In a transport of joy, I landed on liberty ground, and as I advanced into the country, received the acclamation of a grateful people," wrote the gleeful hero of his sweet return to freedom.

Some New Hampshire Grants residents joined the colonists to fight the British during the Revolutionary War. Others held political conventions to separate from New Hampshire, New York, and Great Britain. On January 14, 1777, at a convention in Westminster, the people of the Grants adopted their own declaration of independence and established an independent republic. Five months later, its name was approved: Vermont, from the French words for "green mountain" (*vert mont*).

It was not until March 4, 1791, that the independent Republic of Vermont became Vermont, the 14th state of the United States of America.

George Washington at Valley Forge, Pennsylvania.
Ethan visited Washington there after his release
by the British. Washington was very impressed
with Ethan's courage.

Last
Wolf Hunt

nstead of heading straight for his home and family, Ethan first visited George Washington at Valley Forge in Pennsylvania. The general and his army were recuperating after a long, tough winter. General Washington cordially welcomed the former leader of the Green Mountain Boys. Washington later described the unique backwoodsman to a friend: "There is an original something in him that commands admiration; and his long captivity and sufferings have only served to increase if possible, his enthusiastic zeal."

Soon after this meeting, Ethan was awarded an

official army commission as a full colonel. He had wanted this military appointment for a long time. But his commission was in the reserve army. And because Congress never called upon his services, Ethan continued to fight for independence and liberty on his own terms.

After three days at the colonial army headquarters, Ethan traveled to Connecticut, where he learned that his brothers Heman and Zimri had recently died. Cousin Remember Baker was also dead. Mary and the children had moved north to Sunderland to live with Ira.

On May 31, 1778, Ethan rode his horse into Bennington, where he was welcomed with much joy and fanfare. Before his arrival, a rumor had spread among the townspeople that it was Ethan, not Heman, who had died. So, in his typical legendary larger-than-life style, the returning hero was also returning from the dead. The town held a huge celebration: a 14-gun salute was fired off–13 shots for the 13 American colonies and 1 for the independent Republic of

Ethan's letter to General George Washington, dated May 18, 1778. Ethan signed the letter as a colonel–his new army rank.

Vermont–and three old cannons were loudly discharged. In light of the fact that it was wartime and military supplies were scarce, the multi-gun salute was an unusually extravagant honor. Ethan so enjoyed the day-long party at the Catamount that he vowed to celebrate the last day of May in Bennington on an annual basis. True to form, Ethan kept his word.

At Ira's place, Ethan found his wife and three daughters well cared for by his bachelor brother, who had become prosperous and influential in the new Republic of Vermont. The owner of a successful gristmill, a busy sawmill, and lots of land, Ira had become a public figure in Vermont, one of the half-dozen men most responsible for developing the new republic's government. Appointed Vermont's first councilor, treasurer, secretary of state (unofficial), and, later, surveyor general, Ira had been chosen to write the introduction to the republic's constitution.

Ethan soon joined his brother and the other officers of the young republic in working to protect Vermont from **annexation** or seizure by New York, New Hampshire, and Great Britain. Over the next several years, Ethan served as a powerful and popular political leader of the independent republic. Historians now believe that the state of Vermont would not exist if it had not been for the influential efforts of Ethan.

In a small farmhouse he rented just down the hill from the Catamount, Ethan wrote and published pro-Vermont political letters, essays, and pamphlets. He attended the local political assemblies and frequently rode his horse to Philadelphia to petition the Continental Congress. Ethan and the other leaders of Vermont were kept especially busy by their old enemy—New York. New York officials continued to lay claim to the land along the eastern border, refusing to even acknowledge what they scornfully referred to as "the pretended state of Vermont."

A Green Mountain Boys–style state militia was formed, and Ethan was elected as the commanding general. When necessary, Ethan would round up his men, riding through the countryside while calling out the old battle cry, "Come, my boys, it's another wolf hunt." Between 1779 and 1784, General Allen and the Vermont militia stormed into a number of Vermont towns where

Yorker sentiments were clearly in evidence.

No one was ever hurt and no shots were ever fired when Ethan's regiment marched into a township where residents had been openly revolting against the new republic. But all protesters were rapidly frightened into submission, and the more prominent Yorkers and rioters were promptly arrested and fined.

Outraged by what they believed to be Vermont's unlawful behavior, the New York authorities constantly threatened to send in their own military forces. Although they never followed through on their threats, the New York governor consistently blocked all attempts by Ethan and the Vermont Assembly to win congressional approval for inclusion with the other colonies as an official American state.

Meanwhile, New Hampshire was petitioning Congress to allow it to annex Vermont. And Great Britain was attempting to entice the outcast Republic of Vermont into joining the British empire. Somehow, despite the ongoing

The Vermont State House. To stay an independent republic, Vermonters had to stand up to Great Britain—as well as New York and New Hampshire.

threats and the devastations of a long war, the young Republic of Vermont held fast. Historians credit Ethan, with his blustery essays and militia attacks, as being the strongest single force in maintaining the integrity of Vermont—an independent republic threatened from all sides but, ultimately, victim to none.

In the spring of 1782, Ethan's third brother, Heber, died. In June of the following year, Mary Allen died of tuberculosis, which was then called consumption. Ethan's oldest daughter, Loraine, died a few months later. Suddenly, Ethan had three young children to take care of. He moved back home to Sunderland. Unable to limit himself to farm chores and housework, Ethan decided to focus his energies on writing the book that he and his old friend Dr. Young had started some 20 years earlier.

Dr. Young had died in 1777. Young's widow passed on to Ethan the beginnings of the book the two friends had developed together. From the unfinished manuscript and the many pages of notes preserved with it, Ethan was able to produce what is still regarded as a masterpiece, *Reason the Only Oracle of Man*. Published in 1785, the book—often referred to as "Allen's Bible"—

was brilliant, wildly unique, and highly contro-versial. Although it didn't make very much money, *Reason* created quite a public stir as the first major work published in the Western Hemisphere to openly debate official Christian doctrine.

In February 1784, at age 46, Ethan married again. His new wife was a beautiful, sophisti-cated, and witty widow, 24-year-old Fanny Montresor Buchanan. Unlike his first, Ethan's second marriage was extremely fulfilling, and the happy husband remained at home to enjoy it. Older and blissfully wed, the adventurous frontiersman spent the remaining years of his life as a Vermont family man and farmer. Fanny bore him three more children, including a son they named Ethan Jr.

For three years the Allens rented lodging in Bennington—near the Catamount, of course. Then they moved north to Burlington in 1787, where Ethan had been building them a modest house. Land-rich and cash-poor, the Allens joined nearly a hundred other families struggling to tame the harsh wilderness in northern Vermont.

Ethan's first harvest was a disappointing one due to the difficult weather. Ethan and his large family were not faring well in the winter of 1789 when he took his ox-drawn hayrack across frozen Lake Champlain on an icy errand. Upon stopping at a cousin's farm to pick up a loan of some much-needed hay, 51-year-old Ethan fell into a coma from which he never awoke. He died shortly thereafter.

On February 16, 1789, four days after his death, Ethan's legendary life was celebrated in a grand and elaborate ceremony held in Burlington. People from all across Vermont, including many of the high officials of the new republic, ventured out in the bitter cold to pay their respects to a true hero. During the military funeral, General Ethan Allen was honored with drum rolls, cannon booms, and musket salutes.

Sometime after 1850, Ethan's gravestone disappeared. By this time, the early Vermont leader had become a full-fledged folk hero, so the state legislature voted to erect a 42-foot granite monument on the grave. In attempting to determine the exact location of the long-buried remains, the gravesite and all of the surrounding area were carefully excavated. No trace of the body or coffin could be found, and the mystery remains unsolved to this day. In death as in life, Ethan managed to be a legend—in his own time, and for all time.

Ethan's last home lies two miles north of Burlington, Vermont's largest city. State historian Ralph Nading Hill discovered the long-forgotten 18th-century building and began its restoration. Now a museum, the Ethan Allen Homestead remains the only historical artifact identified with the Vermont hero. The exact location of his grave was lost long ago.

GLOSSARY

annexation–incorporation of territory into an existing state or country

Calvinism–doctrine of religious leader John Calvin, who broke from the Roman Catholic Church in the 1500s to form his own sect; his followers eventually produced the Presbyterian Church

carillon–bells in a tower, usually a church

catamount–mountain lion; large, graceful wildcat also known as the puma or panther

civilian–nonmilitary person

felicity–great happiness or bliss; good fortune

frontier–undeveloped region just beyond a settled area

garrison–military post

grog–old-fashioned alcoholic drink made with rum and water

militia–a group of men who are called to serve in the military in emergencies

minutemen–Yankee militiamen who, during the Revolutionary War, pledged to be ready to fight the British on a moment's notice

musket–shoulder gun used from the late 1500s through the 1700s

patriot–person devoted to his or her country; name used for Americans who favored independence during the Revolutionary War

Puritan—an English Protestant of the 1700s who was extremely devout and strict, regarding all material pleasure and luxury as sinful

scurvy—disease caused by a lack of vitamin C

smelting—process of removing iron from rock taken from mines

squatters—people who live on a piece of land in an attempt to win ownership without owning title to the property

township—crude frontier hamlet, often consisting of a few families and, typically, a tavern and a place of worship

wicket-gate—smaller gate built into a larger gate or doorway

Yankee—person who lives in New England; name used for American patriots during the Revolutionary War

Yorkers—people who lived in New York or sided with the New York governor during the real-estate conflict of the 1700s in the Grants

CHRONOLOGY

1738	Born on January 21 in Litchfield, Connecticut.
1739	Family moves to Cornwall, Connecticut.
1755	Father Joe Allen dies; Ethan's formal studies end as he assumes his father's duties.
1757	Joins a militia but misses the action in the French and Indian War.
1761	Founds the first iron-smelting industry in Connecticut.
1762	Marries Mary Brownson.
1763	Moves to Salisbury, Connecticut; befriends Dr. Thomas Young.
1767	Moves the family to Sheffield, Massachusetts; takes a solo trek through the New Hampshire Grants.
1770	Purchases first two plots of land in the Grants.
1771	The Green Mountain Boys form, electing Ethan as leader; a reward is offered by New York for Ethan's capture.
1775–76	On March 13, the Westminster Massacre takes place in the Grants; the battles of Lexington and Concord launch the Revolutionary War in April; Ethan leads the capture of Fort Ticonderoga on May 10; is captured by the British in Montreal on September 25; is kept in captivity on British ships and in foreign jails as a prisoner of war.

1777	Jailed in British-held New York City; the Grants declares itself the independent Republic of Vermont.
1778	Is released on May 6; returns to the northland to assist Vermont in retaining independence.
1781	British surrender at Yorktown, Virginia.
1783	Treaty of Paris officially ends the Revolutionary War; wife Mary Allen dies.
1784	Marries Fanny Buchanan.
1785	*Reason the Only Oracle of Man* is published.
1787	The Allens settle in Burlington, Vermont.
1789	Dies at home on February 12.
1791	Vermont becomes the 14th American state.

REVOLUTIONARY WAR TIME LINE ━━

1765 The Stamp Act is passed by the British. Violent protests against it break out in the colonies.

1766 Britain ends the Stamp Act.

1767 Britain passes a law that taxes glass, painter's lead, paper, and tea in the colonies.

1770 Five colonists are killed by British soldiers in the Boston Massacre.

1773 People are angry about the taxes on tea. They throw boxes of tea from ships in Boston Harbor into the water. It ruins the tea. The event is called the Boston Tea Party.

1774 The British pass laws to punish Boston for the Boston Tea Party. They close Boston Harbor. Leaders in the colonies meet to plan a response to these actions.

1775 The Battles of Lexington and Concord begin the American Revolution.

1776 The Declaration of Independence is signed. France and Spain give money to help the Americans fight Britain. Nathan Hale is captured by the British. He is charged with being a spy and is executed.

1777 Leaders choose a flag for America. The American troops win some important battles over the British. General Washington and his troops spend a very cold, hungry winter in Valley Forge.

1778 France sends ships to help the Americans win the war. The British are forced to leave Philadelphia.

1779 French ships head back to France. The French support the Americans in other ways.

1780 Americans discover that Benedict Arnold is a traitor. He escapes to the British. Major battles take place in North and South Carolina.

1781 The British surrender at Yorktown.

1783 A peace treaty is signed in France. British troops leave New York.

1787 The U.S. Constitution is written. Delaware becomes the first state in the Union.

1789 George Washington becomes the first president. John Adams is vice president.

FURTHER READING

Alderman, Clifford Lindsey. *The Dark Eagle: The Story of Benedict Arnold.* New York: Macmillan, 1976.

Collier, Christopher. *The American Revolution 1763–1783.* New York: Benchmark Books, 1998.

Hahn, Michael T. *Ethan Allen: A Life of Adventure.* Shelburne, Vt.: New England Press, 1994.

Holbrook, Stewart H. *America's Ethan Allen.* Boston: Houghton Mifflin, 1949.

McDowell, Bart. *The Revolutionary War: America's Fight for Freedom.* Washington, D.C.: National Geographic Society, 1967.

McNair, Sylvia. *America the Beautiful: Vermont.* Chicago: Children's Press, 1991.

Meltzer, Milton, ed. *The American Revolutionaries: A History in Their Own Words, 1750–1800.* New York: Thomas Y. Crowell, 1987.

Pelta, Kathy. *Hello U.S.A.: Vermont.* Minneapolis, Minn.: Lerner Publishing Company, 1994.

Wade, Mary Dodson. *Benedict Arnold.* New York: Franklin Watts, 1994.

INDEX

PICTURE CREDITS

ABOUT THE AUTHOR ══════

VIRGINIA ARONSON is the author of more than two dozen books, including a number of biographies for young adults. While attending college at the University of Vermont, she rooted for their fierce hockey team, the Catamounts. Now she lives in South Florida with her writer husband and their young son, who has yet to see a green mountain.

Senior Consulting Editor **ARTHUR M. SCHLESINGER, JR.** is the leading American historian of our time. He won the Pulitzer Prize for his book *The Age of Jackson* (1945), and again for *A Thousand Days* (1965). This chronicle of the Kennedy Administration also won a National Book Award. He has written many other books, including a multi-volume series, *The Age of Roosevelt*. Professor Schlesinger is the Albert Schweitzer Professor of the Humanities at the City University of New York, and has been involved in several other Chelsea House projects, including the COLONIAL LEADERS series of biographies on the most prominent figures of early American history.